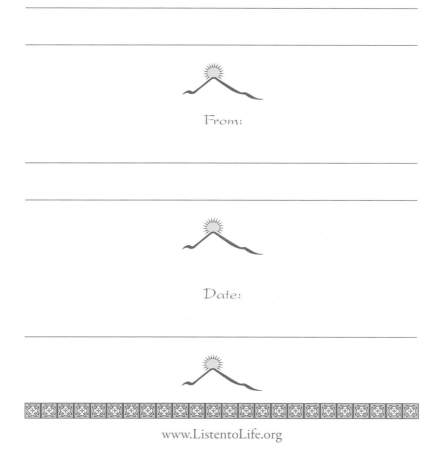

Presented To:

From:

Date:

www.ListentoLife.org

Listen to Life with Your Pet

The Pet Lover's Guide to a Positive Life

Listen to life and make a positive life, not just a living, in a negative world.

www.ListentoLife.org

ISBN 0-9715074-3-0

Library of Congress Control Number 2001012345

First Edition

Cover design and layout: Rebecca Fitzgerald   www.graphicdesignsthatfitz.com
Promotional photo: Patrick Jinks   www.jinksperspective.com

www.ListentoLife.org

For our daughter, Elizabeth
who goes to college this fall.
Thanks for teaching me how to love like our pets
unconditionally.

Contents

LISTEN TO LIFE WITH YOUR DOG

LISTEN TO LIFE WITH YOUR CAT

LISTEN TO LIFE WITH YOUR HORSE

Listen to Life with Your Pet

The Pet Lover's Guide to a Positive Life

*Listen to life and make a positive life,
not just a living, in a negative world.*

www.ListentoLife.org

Introduction

I didn't grow up with a pet.

Unless you count Goldie the goldfish.

When I was born, I had allergies and asthma so severe that everyone but my two doctors and parents gave up on my living a normal life. That meant a furry pet with dander made me sneeze until I couldn't breathe, and since breathing is necessary for living, my parents decided not to risk it.

So I didn't grow up with a pet.

That is, if you measure growing up in terms of years. But if growing up is a lifelong process that defies the mile markers of years, I am growing up with pets. In fact, you might say that other than my daughters, I have learned more about what it means to make a positive life in a negative world from our pets than anyone else.

As I write this, Jake barks through my open window. He's one of our five yellow Labrador retrievers. The others are Princess, Dutchess, Countessa, and Lady Lucy. Then there's the miniature schnauzer, Rags, whom I nicknamed "Bud" because being the smallest he has enough of a complex without enduring the name Rags. These "family members" were preceded by yellow Labs Charlie and Cody and the queen-beagle-in-charge, Maxie.

As I look out over our farm, across the pastures, I see our quarter horses, Sugar, Seeker, and Leo. If you get to the pearly gates and St. Pete offers you a chance to come back, ask to be one of my family's horses. "Pasture ornaments," I call them. They're the largest, spoiled rotten babies on the planet. So were Sissy and Jay Bird before them. Some days I wish I had their life. Make that most days.

Then, reclining on the bench near the old farm house chimney, surveying his kingdom is Boo Radley the cat. Yes, all of it belongs to him, but he has yet to make a payment. That doesn't stop him from acting as if it's his. Boo adopted us, you see, and patiently allows us to live with him . . . just as Samantha, Penelope, Maybelle, and Norman did before him.

How did I come to be adopted by all of these pets? Listening to my story, some would say the miracle of modern medicine, but I would say the miracle of a divine gift . . . and not just a physical one, either. Really, more of a spiritual one.

That's why I wrote this book—to share the life gift I'm receiving from our pets with you: how to make a positive life, not just a living, in this negative world.

You and I have a lot in common:
- We love our pets.
- We treat our pets like our children and sometimes better than our spouses.
- We receive far more from our pets than we ever give them.

I recently read that about three-fourths of married pet owners greet their pet first when they come home. I thought, *That can't be right*, until I remembered that Princess greets me first as I walk in the door.

Also, I read recently that about two-thirds of pet owners celebrate their pets' birthdays and give them presents at holidays. I thought, *That can't be right*, until I remembered that our dogs, cat, and horses all have Christmas stockings.

Then I read recently that over half of all pet owners turn on music for their pet. Again I thought, *That can't be right*, until I remembered that I installed a stereo system in our horse barn for the horses.

We do love our pets, don't we?

Someone asked me once what my life goal is. I thought for a moment and then said, "I want to be the man that my dogs think I am."

Now if you're a cat lover, your fur is bristling, your back is arched, and you might be spitting. Not to worry. A section in this book has been written just for you, and every story is about cats. So settle down, knead a little, and purr.

If you're a horse lover, you're probably stomping around, snorting, and standing up on your hind legs. Well, when you're through showing off, look for the section in this book in which every story is about horses. Just calm yourself, stick your head in the feed bucket, and nicker.

Oh, and not that you dog lovers were concerned, but there's an entire belly-rubbing, head-scratching, ball-fetching section for you. After all, you are the ones dubbed "best friend" so you have more stories than the others.

Regardless of which pet you love more, all of these stories are about how our pets help us discover ways to make a positive life, not just a living, in this negative world. That's a meaning hidden from many of us today but not from our pets. Life does get rather complicated at times, doesn't it?

We allow the noise of life to drown out the music. We focus more on the negative than the positive. We expect to pop a pill and cure our ills.

As I'm growing up with our pets, I'm discovering that if I listen to life with them, if I approach life like my dogs, cats, and horses do, then the complications aren't so loud, and the meanings emerge more clearly. I'm more positive as I make a life. As I'm growing up with our pets, I find myself at mid-life understanding that the same Creator who knit me together shaped and breathed life into them. That we share life together and I can learn from them a fuller, richer, more positive meaning of how life is to be enjoyed.

Isn't that why you're so crazy about your pet, too? You make a positive life together? The stress melts away as your cat purrs. Or the distress eases as you throw the ball for your dog to fetch. Or the problem compress wrapped around your throat loosens as you gallop on your horse.

So yes, I am still growing up, only now with my pets. They're teaching me how to make a positive life in a negative world. This book is filled with our stories.

We hope these stories grow you closer to your pet so you will listen to life with your pet and make a positive life, not just a living, in this negative world.

Joey Faucette   Jake   Princess   Dutchess   Lucy   Tessa   Rags aka Bud

Leo   Sugar   Seeker   Boo Radley

Dogs

Dutchess and her favorite ball

*"If there are no dogs in heaven,
then when I die I want to go where they went."*

Will Rogers

Do all dogs really go to heaven?

Shortly after I talked my wife into marrying me, I entered graduate school. It was this wonderful, ivory-tower-anchored, theory-filled world which did little to prepare me for a conversation with her one day about whether all dogs go to heaven.

"Of course not," I said with all of the smug assurance of someone armed with just enough theological knowledge to be dangerous to everyone in a 100-mile radius.

"All I know is that Pandora (her childhood German shepherd) is going to jump up on me and lick my face as soon as I walk in," she said.

Life has a way of redefining the reality of conversations like this one. Cody, a yellow Labrador retriever, came to live with us. He had this way of being around you that was quite comforting. Cody lived from a peaceful place within.

As the years ran quickly by, Cody's body followed. He couldn't stand to go outside to the bathroom. Our vet said there was nothing she could do. Cody was an old man now and headed for another life. Still, I wasn't sure that all dogs go to heaven . . . until one day we decided that Cody had suffered enough. I went down to the basement kennel, picked him up, and said, "Old Man, you've had enough. The vet is coming to put you to sleep. Where do you want to go?"

Cody walked slowly outside around our home and up the path to the horse barn. He struggled up the hill and through the horse barn.

As he stepped out of the barn, he took a couple of steps and stared off across the horizon. In the distance was Smith Mountain, standing tall yet gracefully against the Carolina blue sky. Cody stood on the exact piece of earth that I had declared on numerous occasions as "the most beautiful spot on this farm."

"Is this it, Old Man?" I asked.

He flopped down, saying, "Yes, this is it."

The vet came to our farm and walked up to where Cody and our family waited. "Say good-bye to Cody," she told us.

His dark brown eyes met mine and said, "I'll see you again."

Cody gave me his peaceful place within.

As he slipped away to sleep, I decided that my wife is right.

All dogs really do go to heaven, a most peaceful place.

Are you enjoying a positive life?

At one time my office was on our farm. One window overlooked our backyard where our yellow Labs play.

I sat one day, writing a story for you, when I heard the puppies barking, playing, and having a great time. I smiled, wishing I was with them. Just then I heard a sound I didn't recognize so I looked up from my laptop to see what it was.

Evidently when my wife fed the Labs that morning, she left one of the metal food pans in a pup's kennel. The puppy had brought it out, flipped it upside down, and discovered how much fun it was to push it all over the yard with her nose. Her sisters thought it looked like fun as well.

As they each took a turn pushing it around the yard, they would suddenly stop, lie down, and put a paw on the pan. Almost as if to say, "Nanny! Nanny Boo-Boo! You can't have it!" Her sisters then stood around barking at her until one of them reached out a paw, flipped the pan out, and was off to another game of Keep Away.

Yes, my wife left the pan out accidentally. But you couldn't convince those puppies of that. I'm sure they saw the pan as a gift from above! These puppies were having the time of their young lives simply by pushing a pan around the yard.

As I watched them, I thought, *Wouldn't it be great if all of us enjoyed the simple pleasures of a positive life like that? Had a ball just pushing a pan around?*

What "accidentally" was left out recently for you to enjoy?

Green lights all the way to work?

A great song on the radio?

A surprise "just because" card that arrives in the mail?

There definitely is more to life than you and I can manipulate or anticipate. Creating fun from accidents births simple pleasures for us to enjoy.

So look around your kennel. Listen to your life and discover everything you need to make a positive life.

Listen to Life with Your Pet

1. Remember a recent time when something happened that you didn't see coming and you had fun because of it.

2. What was your mood like? How did you feel? What were you thinking at the time?

3. What will you do differently today to listen to your positive life and discover a pan lying around?

Life changes fast, doesn't it?

I still remember when we brought Jake the yellow Labrador retriever home. He was such a cute little guy, but almost from the minute he arrived, he started growing really fast.

He grew so quickly that pretty soon he had these huge paws and these long, floppy ears. So every time he tried to run anywhere, he got so excited that he tumbled, his big paws tripping over those floppy ears. We all had a good laugh at him, but it didn't seem to bother Jake.

The challenge for Jake was that he was growing so fast, he couldn't keep up. His mind couldn't adapt to his body's changes quickly enough to send the message, "Here's how you run." Still he just kept getting up and running, even learning to slap his ear away with his paw as he ran.

Just as with Jake, life changes that fast for you, doesn't it?

Just when you think you've figured out how to do something at work, a new computer program is introduced, or a different system is put in place. You tumble.

Or you discover what works best in your relationship with your spouse, then something changes. You can't adapt quickly enough. You trip.

Or you decide to change your nutrition plan and exercise more, only to find out that your child's soccer practice is at the same time as your fitness center schedule so it's fast food and sitting. You stumble again.

So how do you get back on your feet while dealing with change at the speed of life?

Jake persevered. He kept going. He didn't stop trying. You can, too.

Jake adapted. He learned to slap his ear away so he wouldn't trip. You can, too.

Jake contextualized. Somehow he knew his situation was temporary. You can, too.

Listen to Life with Your Pet

1. Name your situation that is changing at the speed of life. See it ending at some fixed point whether it's two weeks, two months, or two years.

2. Ponder your changing challenge and discover how you can adapt to it most effectively.

3. What will you need to persevere?

Are you ready for an opportunity?

I was cleaning up around our farm. We had done some remodeling, and I was loading up the scrap materials into the truck bed to take off to the dumpster. I couldn't get everything on the truck so I knew I'd have to make two trips.

One of our yellow labs, Cody, was helping me. You know, keeping me company by walking with me as I carried each load. He sniffed around to see who had worked there. He even found a small scrap of wood and lay down to gnaw on it for a while. I guess that was his version of recycling.

Since he was so helpful, I offered him a ride down the road to the dumpster. I opened the door, he hopped in, and away we went. He wanted to drive. At least I suppose that's what he wanted as he tried to sit in my lap, but soon he settled in on the passenger seat, content to stick his head out the window and air out his ears.

We returned home, I let Cody out and began filling the second load. Before I embarked on this trip, Jake, who was a puppy then, barked at me like he wanted to go, too. So when I finished loading, I brought him over to the truck, opened the door, and he wouldn't get in. He was, after all, just a puppy, and the only time he left the farm was to go to the vet's office to get stuck with a needle or that cold, round thing stuck on his chest. So he wouldn't get in the truck.

Are you like Jake sometimes? You think you want to do something until you have the opportunity? Then you won't get in?

Like Jake, maybe you've had a previous experience that wasn't so positive. That memory keeps you from getting into the opportunity.

Like Jake, perhaps you're more in love with the idea of the opportunity than doing what it takes to jump up into it.

Like Jake, maybe you just want to do it because someone else is.

Whatever your reason for hesitating, how will you get ready for the opportunity to enjoy a positive life today?

Listen to Life with Your Pet

1. What opportunity is currently presenting itself to you to make your life more positive?

2. Discover your reason for hesitating by being surgically honest with yourself. Use the three possibilities above to prompt your personal discovery mission.

3. See yourself more like Cody than Jake. Visualize yourself as having already taken advantage of the opportunity. How is life more positive? What benefits are you enjoying?

Want to party?

I t's a massive understatement to say that our family is crazy about our pets. We live on a farm just so we can have more of them.

Because we're so in love with our pets, you can imagine our reaction when Cody and Jake, two of our yellow Labrador retrievers, escaped the backyard fence and didn't come back home all day. We were really concerned. In fact, we panicked.

Our minds raced to a thousand possible scenarios, each one worse than the other. We saw Cody and Jake dead on the road, picked up by someone who stole them, and lots of other worst-case outcomes.

You can also imagine our reaction when these two prodigal dogs showed back up at home later that evening. First we made sure they were fine. Then when they were, we wanted to scold them. Instead, we had a party. We were so glad to see them. We scratched them all over and loved on them, fed them, gave them treats, and hugged them . . . all inside the backyard fence, of course. It was quite a celebration!

Have you ever had a similar experience, only with a person? Someone who went lost, then was found?

Maybe it was your friend—the two of you had a disagreement and left each other for a while, but then you got back together.

Perhaps it was your spouse—somehow one of you strayed away and got lost but found your way back home.

Or it could have been your child—assaulted by confusion and chaos.

Who hasn't run away from home as a child? Only to return when you come to your senses?

How did you react when this person was found?

- Scolding? "What were you thinking? Oh wait, you weren't!"
- Guilt? "How could you do this to me?"
- Constant reminding? "Don't think I've forgotten. I'll never trust you again."

Instead, try throwing a party. Go ahead and look past the incident and love up on the person. Just be grateful that she is fine. Just give thanks for his well-being.

And enjoy making your life positive!

Listen to Life with Your Pet

1. Who was lost to you?

2. When they returned, how did you react?

3. Based on this story, how do you wish you had reacted? How will your wish remind you the next time someone you care about is lost?

Are you cool?

My wife put out a water bowl in the backyard for our yellow Labrador retriever, Jake, when he was a puppy. He drank a little water out of it, then, being a Lab and loving water, tried to get in it. Of course, he turned it over immediately, spilling all the water. He stood back and looked like, "What happened? Who spilled the water?"

Next my wife put out a five-gallon bucket full of water for Jake, placing it in a milk crate, hoping to secure it better. What did Jake do? Drank a little, put both front paws in it, and pulled it over, spilling all the water—again. And again, he just stood there, wondering, "What happened?"

So my wife bought a plastic kiddy pool and filled it with water, thinking that Jake could now both get in it and drink from it. Guess what he did? He chewed holes in the hard-plastic sides of the pool, and all the water leaked out. And one more time Jake just did not understand what the problem was—himself.

Sometimes I'm like Jake.

All I have to do is enjoy the cool refreshment of the positive in the negative heat of life. It is there for the asking. I have more than I need and everything I want.

But I don't make the choice just to enjoy. I spill it, or pull it over, or mess it up. Then I wonder, "What happened?" or blame life—"It's not fair." All the while, I don't connect my actions with the results. I avoid responsibility for my behavior.

What about you?

Do you ever have an experience like Jake or me?

Life is positively more fulfilling, packed with meaning, and richer when you enjoy what you receive as it's given rather than trying to do more with it than is intended. Each positive gift presents itself as it is for you to enjoy.

So just lap up the positive today and stay cool in the negative heat of your life.

Listen to Life with Your Pet

1. Recall an experience in which you attempted to make more of something than it was meant to be.

2. How did that work for you?

3. Name specific actions you can do differently next time, choosing to drink deeply of the positive as it presents itself.

Do you make the most of change?

We built some new dog kennels in our backyard. They're a nice size for the yellow Labs we raise, but one of them, Jake, just wasn't quite accustomed to it. So he barked and paced for a few days while it was his turn to remain inside. He didn't appreciate the change in his routine.

Well, after those few days, I noticed that Jake was quiet during the time in his kennel. I wondered what had changed so I looked at him when he wasn't noticing. Jake had taken a ball, his favorite ball, from the yard and brought it in his kennel. There he was, tossing the ball up in the air and catching it in his mouth. Then he threw it against the fence and pounced on the rebound.

He reminded me of when I was a little boy and baseball was my life. When my younger brother didn't want to play catch and my dad wasn't home, I would stand in the backyard, toss my baseball just as high up in the air as I could, and then catch it. Next I would hurl it as hard as I could against the brick wall of our home, pretending to be Willie Mays throwing out someone from deep center field.

Something will change in your world today. You can count on it. I promise it will happen.

Odds are you will not like the change. You didn't ask for it. You didn't see it coming. You resent it.

You'll face a choice: complain and pace or adapt and make the most of it.

If you choose to complain and pace, understand that plenty of people will join you, but you will not make a positive life.

If you choose to adapt and make the most of it like Jake, know that you may be going it alone at times, but you will make a positive life.

What will you choose to do with the change in your life today?

Choose to make the most of it as you listen to life and make a positive life.

Listen to Life with Your Pet

1. What changed in your life recently?

2. How did you react to the change?

3. What can you choose to do with the change to be more like Jake?

How's your voice?

We have a lot of dogs around our home. We have our five yellow Labrador retrievers who make beautiful puppies that join loving families. Then there is Rags aka Bud the miniature schnauzer. And there are the dogs my wife boards for others while they're out of town. So we have lots of dogs around our place.

Now you might think with that many dogs around, we'd get tired of the barking. However, my wife has this marvelous way with animals that makes them happy, which means there's not a lot of barking. And when the dogs do bark, you might think, Oh, it's just a lot of noise.

It's much more than that. You see, each dog has a unique voice. My wife taught me to listen to certain special qualities that make each dog's voice different, much as our voices are unique. Also, there are particular nuances—like changes in excitement or cadence—that let you know what's going on with that dog whether it's danger or delight, hunger or happiness.

Listening to life so you can make a positive life, not just a living, in a negative world is a lot like listening to our dogs' voices. At first hearing, it's just a lot of noise barking at you, which all sounds the same. It's easy to stop right there and dismiss it all and say something like, "Life is just noisy and negative."

However, life is much more than that. Each person has a unique voice that has certain special qualities that express a personal creativity that is distinctive among the 6.5 billion or so of us here on the planet.

Sure, a lot of these voices carry negative noise. But if you invest the time, energy, and attention to listen—not just hear—you discover a person's desires and dreams, her hopes and happiness, his passion and purpose, their gifts and goals.

From this listening emerges a positive tide of energy that lifts your life's ship. You listen to your own voice and make similar discoveries about yourself. You resist the urge to compare and compete and instead cooperate and complement with others in pursuit of your positive life.

So listen to your life voice . . . and others' as well . . . as you make a positive life.

Listen to Life with Your Pet

1. Listen more intently during your next conversation. Filter out the negative and let the positive flow through.

2. Respond by commenting on the positive aspects of what the person just said.

3. Affirm the positive in the conversation by adding your own unique perspective.

Who do you follow?

Our family absolutely loves raising yellow Labrador retrievers. One day I went out in the backyard where Princess was playing and had started barking. She was young, about a year old, playful, and fun. She was on a lead and had wrapped herself all the way around the tree to the point where she could only lie down. She had no room to move. So she barked for help.

I discovered her dilemma and started just to unhook her, unwrap the lead from around the tree, and then rehook her. Instead, I decided to get her to follow me around the tree however many turns it took to unwrap. I called her name and prompted her to follow me. She did, bounding around the tree, glad to see me, following my "Here, Princess" command. I showed her the way out of her dilemma.

I'm like Princess sometimes, aren't you? I wrap myself into some pretty tight predicaments. Then I cry out for help.

My positive life question then becomes, "Do I follow who shows up to lead me out?"

That's harder to do sometimes than it sounds.

Do you find that to be true for you as you try to make a positive life?

Ego gets in the way, and you hear yourself saying, "I can handle this. I don't need to follow you!" Then how did you get wrapped around this predicament?

Emotions litter the pathway as well, and you feel like "I should be independent enough to do this." If that were the case, how do you feel about what got you into this tight spot?

Unrealistic expectations block the positive journey, too; "This isn't what I thought would happen." You have had other surprises in your life, haven't there?

You will follow someone or something in your life, positive or negative. Will you follow your ego? Your emotions? Your expectations?

Be like Princess. Follow that someone who comes to you whom you recognize as a person invested in your best interest, not just someone who fixes your life. Someone who leads you down the right path, empowering you to be a part of the solution. Such persons are sent to you so you can make a positive life in this negative world.

Listen to Life with Your Pet

1. What was the last tight spot you found yourself in?

2. How did you overcome it?

3. Give thanks right now for the person who was sent to empower you to find your way out.

Got time for love?

A friend came over, and we watched a football game together. He sat on one end of our sofa. Princess, one of our yellow Labrador retrievers, walked into the room, spotted room on the sofa next to him and crawled up.

Within just a few minutes she had her head in his lap, and he was rubbing it. Pretty soon she had her head and shoulders in his lap, and he was rubbing her neck.

The next thing I knew, she was licking his face, and he was rubbing her neck. Then she was trying to get her whole body into his lap. He was laughing, I was laughing, and in her own way Princess was laughing!

Life gets really busy sometimes, doesn't it?

Do you ever hear yourself say something like, "There's no way I can possibly get all of this done"?

Or one appointment runs a little over, and you say, "Who set this schedule so tight? Now I'm behind for the rest of the day!"

Or, "Honey, I'm going to be late again. I have to get this report in by midnight."

Yes, life gets really busy at times. In those times you neglect making a positive life and just make a living. You have no time available to listen to your life, do you?

Here's a little secret I discovered listening to life with Princess that's actually quite huge: if you truly want to make a positive life and not just a living, take some time out to share love with another.

Sure, start slowly at first like Princess did as she crawled up on one end of the sofa. That might mean you stop working 15 minutes earlier today than you did yesterday and go home to your family or out with a friend.

Then inch your way over closer, within reach of your family member or friend. That might look like going into work an hour later one morning to enjoy an extra cup of coffee.

And before you know it, your small steps achieve huge results of a positive life. Your stress melts. Your distress disappears. You are a human being, not a human doing.

Make a positive life today like Princess and discover that when you give a little love to someone else, you receive a lot of love back!

Listen to Life with Your Pet

1. When did you last intentionally stop working and choose to be with someone?

2. How did that single decision move you toward making a positive life, not just a living?

3. What kind of love did you receive back?

Do you persist?

My wife and I have a morning routine. She takes one of our yellow Labs, Princess, out in the morning. I'm inside having my morning quiet time, starting my day by listening to life. When Princess finishes outside, my wife lets her back inside, and I'm supposed to feed her.

One morning recently I was so focused on being quiet and listening that I didn't realize when Princess came back inside. There I sat in my chair, praying and meditating. Now I don't know whether it was 30 seconds or 30 minutes later, I became aware that I was being watched. Actually, stared at is more like it. You know that feeling that you get when someone's eyes are boring holes in you?

I opened my eyes slowly, and there sat Princess at attention, tail wagging, her deep brown eyes staring at me, waiting patiently yet persistently to be fed.

I got up and fixed her food, and as I did, I thought how sometimes I don't wait as well as Princess did. I'm not always patient. Sometimes I don't persist long enough to get what I'm after.

Do you?

Are you patient? Do you wait with patience, believing that timing is everything? Knowing that sooner or later, since there is enough to go around, you will be fed?

Do you persist? Do you continue to believe that you can reach your goal? Knowing that at any moment what you seek will come to you?

The negative world says you should romp and stomp, demanding your rights immediately. You shouldn't have to be patient.

The negative world says you deserve instant gratification, at the front of the line, without exerting too much effort.

The positive life discovers that when you patiently persevere like Princess, you get it all. Don't give up today. Patiently keep after whatever positive goal you have no matter how long the odds. Persist as evidence of your faith that you can make a positive life and not just a living as you listen to life.

Listen to Life with Your Pet

1. When are you most vulnerable to giving up?

2. How have you patiently persisted in these types of situations in the past?

3. Describe how your patient persistence created positivity in your life.

How do you greet your guests?

Our yellow Labrador retriever, Princess, moved from the backyard into our home when our younger daughter had her tonsils removed. Our daughter found great comfort in having Princess in bed with her. So she has been in our home since.

Princess has a really interesting way of greeting our guests, all of whom she is convinced come to see her. She invites them to play with her.

She starts by walking up and standing beside them as they come in the door, her tail wagging, really her whole body shaking, welcoming them in. Next, she stays close by the guest as he comes in and has a seat. Then once the guest sits down, Princess goes to her toy basket, picks up a pull toy, brings it to her new best friend, plops it in the guest's lap, and sits patiently. She waits with hopeful anticipation for the guest to either throw the toy or play tug-of-war. She especially enjoys greeting our daughters' boyfriends this way because they usually play tug-of-war, which she loves. (I wish she would bite the boyfriends, not play with them, but my wife won't let her.)

Do you greet guests like Princess?

Do the people that come to see you or meet you for dinner know how happy you are to see them?

Hospitality is a wonderful gift we extend to one another. It's a positive affirmation that we are welcome in a place by someone. That they anticipated our visit. That they invite us into some activity we can enjoy together. That they are absolutely delighted we came over.

While we do live in a negative world, our positive hospitality becomes a welcome oasis of refreshment. So invite someone over to your home. No, it doesn't matter what shape your home is in. They're coming to see you, not visit a museum. Greet them like Princess. Then watch as all of you create a positive life right there in your own home.

Listen to Life with Your Pet

1. Think of someone you can invite into your home.

2. Imagine them walking in your door. See yourself greeting them. What does that look like?

3. See the reaction on their faces. What does your hospitality positively look like on them?

What's your first reaction?

I'll always remember the first time our family took one of our yellow Labs to the beach. Princess was chosen to go. She loves the water but always had been in a pond or lake. She never had seen the ocean with its breaking waves.

So when we took her down for the first time, she really didn't know what to think. I mean, the ocean's wet so she knew she's supposed to like it, but the crashing waves scared her. This water moved, a lot, and that was different. So she was rather timid at first, playing tag with the tides.

Soon we couldn't get her out of the water. She jumped the waves and loved every minute of it. Then she discovered the sand and in minutes was on her way to China, digging a hole just as quickly as she could, enthralled with how easy it was to dig in this dirt which was totally unlike the hard soil around our home on a mountain.

What is your first reaction when you face a new situation?

Are you like Princess? A bit timid? Perhaps fearful?

Fear of the unknown is a powerful inhibitor to our launching out into the unfamiliar. Many times in our lives we choose the familiar, even if it's miserable for us, over the new simply because we are afraid of what might be.

Are you like Princess? Do you work to overcome your timidity? Try out the unfamiliar situation and discover the beauty of something new? Even finding in it more positive pleasure than what you knew previously?

Sometime soon, maybe even today, you will face your ocean of unfamiliarity. Take a deep breath, and go play in it as you listen to life and make a positive life, not just a living, in this negative world.

Listen to Life with Your Pet

1. What new and unknown situation have you faced recently?

2. What was your first reaction?

3. Was that your final reaction, also?
    Or did you go play in it to discover the positive possibilities?

How do you face a huge task?

Our family raises yellow Labrador retrievers. Princess became mother to ten of the cutest little puppies you've ever seen. This litter was her largest ever so I was curious to see how she would care for them.

Basically she spent the first day or so getting to know each of her puppies, making sure they all nursed enough, and keeping them clean with all systems functioning. Then after a day or so, when she knew each puppy well, she created two shifts for nursing. One group of five nursed while the other group of five slept. Then when it was time to change shifts—which was when the nursing group fell asleep—she got up and moved over to the other group and started nursing them.

Who would have thought that Princess would have created such an efficient distribution of labor that any management expert would have been proud to design?

Princess knows how to make a positive life both for herself and her puppies, doesn't she?

First, she got to know her puppies. That's a great first step to your making a positive life. Get to know the people around you really well whether at home or work or your neighborhood. When you're managing a lot of people, they can all look alike as with Princess's puppies. They might complain about the same things and make similar requests. Yet they are unique. Live positive by celebrating each person.

Second, Princess discovered the best way to meet her puppies' needs.

At first blush, you might think she was a bit hardhearted by making half of the litter wait. Actually, the chaos of ten squirming, squeaking puppies all trying to nurse simultaneously was far more cruel. As the more aggressive pups who nursed first fell asleep, she nudged them away into a group. Then she pulled in the others. Live positive by caring for others on their terms, according to their needs and desires.

Finally, Princess took care of herself. That chaos of ten puppies seeking to feed at once took a toll on her. Raising puppies is a marathon of weeks, not a sprint of hours. She realized the need to use her energy and nutrition strategically so she could best serve her puppies. Live positive by caring for yourself while meeting others' needs.

Listen to Life with Your Pet

1. What huge task are you facing now?

2. What can you learn from Princess?

3. Pick one of her strategies and implement it today.

How much do you trust?

I was sitting on our bed, putting on my shoes. One of our yellow Labs, Princess, was on the floor at my feet. That's where she usually spends the morning as we get ready to go. She just really wants to be with us and enjoys some time stretched out on the floor of our bedroom.

So there she is, lying on the floor, eyes closed. I just couldn't resist. I took my foot, the one without the shoe, and started rubbing her belly ever so softly and gently. She never opened her eyes. She was still, the corner of her mouth turning up ever so slightly, almost like she was smiling.

After about a minute or so, she rolled over a bit for me to rub another part of her belly. She still kept her eyes closed. And pretty soon I was on the floor with her, rubbing her with my hand now, and she still hadn't opened an eye. She totally trusted me to rub her, not hurt her.

Trust is so precious, isn't it?

Whom do you trust the way Princess trusted me? Someone you can close your eyes on, or turn your back on, and not have to be concerned in the least that they have only your best interests in mind?

Anyone come to mind? Jot their name(s) down in the margin.

Now who trusts you the way Princess trusted me? Someone who can close their eyes on you? Turn their back on you? Not have to concern themselves in the least with your motives or intentions being anything but good for them?

Who do you hope that would be? Jot their name(s) down in the margin.

Trust is the currency of exchange in making your positive life.

Want to experience more of the positive life in the midst of this negative world?

Grow your list of people who trust you. Fill the margins of this page and then an entire notebook with the names of people who trust you.

When you do, you discover that your list of people you trust grows exponentially, too.

The positive results you receive in life are in direct proportion to the trust you give.

Listen to Life with Your Pet

1. Who came to you recently asking for your trust?

2. Whom would you like to trust more?

3. How will you multiply your currency of trust?

What do you do when it snows?

Have you ever seen a puppy playing in the first snowfall he's ever seen? It's absolutely hilarious. We had a litter of Lab puppies one winter who were old enough to go outside. I'm not sure who enjoyed the experience more—the puppies or us watching the puppies.

One puppy tried to catch the snow as it hit the ground. Then, when he couldn't do that, he jumped in the air trying to catch the flakes. When he did catch one, of course, it dissolved in his mouth, and he didn't understand where it went.

When the ground was covered, he and his Lab brothers and sisters chased one another in it, sliding around, playing in the snow. They had the time of their young lives.

Now contrast our Labs playing in the snow with people you know. Not you, naturally, but think of others and how they react when it snows. People you know who get grouchy because they can't get out of their driveway. Or whine because their kids are missing another day of school, which might cut into their summer vacation. Or stand in long grocery store lines for milk and bread? (With a wife and two daughters at home, I always stood in line for toilet paper!)

So who makes a more positive life when it snows, Labrador retriever puppies or the people you know?

Mark Twain once said something like, "The weather is the most discussed and least acted on subject known to us."

Or, to put it another way, you can't do anything about the weather. So when it snows, enjoy yourself. Play in it. Invite your friends. Avoid grouchy people so you aren't like them. Don't forecast despair into the future at the expense of the present enjoyable moment.

Live positive like a Lab puppy in the present moment, come what may.

Listen to Life with Your Pet

1. What recently changed in your life that was totally beyond your control?

2. How did you react to it—like a Lab puppy or someone you know?

3. What can you learn from that experience about how to live positive?

Who are you?

By now you've discovered that I really prefer yellow Labrador retrievers. Although my wife whom I love dearly is a brunette, it seems to me that in the canine world, blondes do have more fun.

However, we have had a dog other than a yellow Lab. In fact, when she was a child, our older daughter wanted "her own dog," a dog other than a yellow Lab.

That was why Santa Claus brought us Maxie one Christmas. Maxie was the runt of her beagle litter, a timid puppy cowering in the corner of the pen when my wife picked her out. All of the other beagles were at the gate, jumping and barking, "Pick me! Pick me!" Not Maxie. She huddled up with herself in the corner, not daring to bark lest she attract attention to herself. She hardly looked up, not quite fitting in with her beagle brothers and sisters. And that's why my wife selected her. "She needs our love," she said.

To say that Maxie responded well to our love would be like saying . . . well, pick your own cliché. She loved our love.

In her day she was the queen of the farm, or so she thought. She strutted around as if she owned the place, keeping the Labs in line, at the back of the line, of course.

What amused me most was that evidently Maxie was a Lab trapped in a beagle's body. Remember how she didn't seem to belong with the other beagles? That's because she really wasn't a beagle.

She was raised with Labs who love to retrieve balls and bumpers. She would sit at your feet, wait for you to throw the ball or bumper, run to get it, retrieve it, drop it at your feet, and wag her tail for you to do it again. She forgot she was a beagle, or maybe she never really was. Maxie discovered her life's identity as a Labrador retriever.

Can you relate to Maxie? Are there times in your life where you just don't seem to fit in? Like you don't belong?

One of the keys to making a positive life is to explore your fit—who you are, what you enjoy doing, what you're good at, what energizes you, what captures your imagination and ignites your passion and purpose. Sometimes that means stepping outside of what appears to fit you, just like Maxie.

Explore your fit and make a positive life, not just a living, in the negative world.

Listen to Life with Your Pet

1. Recall the last time you woke up and asked yourself, "Why am I doing this today?"

2. What did you decide?

3. In the space below, write down one activity you want to try that's different from what you'll do today. Put a close deadline on it and tell a friend you trust who will later ask you what your experience was like.

Do you sometimes just run in circles?

A window in my former office looks up a small mountain over the backyard where our dogs play. I sat, writing these stories one day, and glanced out the window to see what the dogs were doing. We raise yellow Labrador retrievers so all of our dogs are yellow Labs except Maxie the beagle who acts more like a Lab than a beagle . . . at least most of the time.

Well, this particular day, Queen Maxie led the other dogs in their morning calisthenics. That morning the activity was running in circles. Now that's something beagles do naturally because they chase rabbits and rabbits run in circles. But Labrador retrievers don't naturally run in circles.

The Labs tried to run in circles. They really did. But Jake couldn't get it right. He kept breaking ranks. He wanted to play with Maxie but just couldn't grasp the concept of a circle. Jake's natural gift was to work in straight lines, running and swimming after downed ducks and geese.

So he insisted on cutting off Maxie in mid-circle, running straight at her. Finally, through sheer determination and exertion of her will, Maxie helped Jake understand how to play—chasing her in a circle, not cutting across to catch her. She coached him to learn that they weren't working a retrieve but playing a game of chase.

Sometimes making a positive life isn't about just getting the job done in a straight line. Sure, making a living is an important part of getting along in the world today. Without it your basic needs aren't met, much less your wants and desires.

But sometimes you just have to run in circles. At least occasionally, set aside your need to be so serious and just have fun. Such fun leads you back to making a positive life!

Listen to Life with Your Pet

1. If I asked your family if you're a fun person, what would they say?

2. When was the last time you did something just for fun? With no purpose for profit other than making a positive life? What was that like for you?

3. How can you create a similar fun experience sometime soon?

Having trouble settling down?

A dog came over to board with us for a week while his owners were on vacation. He was a young one and evidently hadn't been away from his home much. He had a little trouble settling down. He walked around, looking for his owners, whined, and generally looked out of sorts.

Whenever a dog comes to our place to stay with us, my wife asks the owners to bring a towel or favorite toy or some bedding, anything that smells like home and is familiar. So since this little fellow was having troubling settling in, my wife put his towel in the kennel with him. He sniffed it all over, began wagging his tail, picked it up, carried it around like a gold medal, and settled right down, enjoying himself from that moment on.

You sometimes find yourself in a strange place, don't you?

Perhaps you travel on business, which means you are in a different city or country each night of the week.

Maybe you recently went off to college, which means you're not only in a strange room in a strange city, but you're with a strange person, or at least one you hardly know.

Or it could be that you and your spouse divorced after being married forever, and your strange place is making plans for dinner as a single person.

Whatever your strange place, you're wondering what's going on, just as this dog did.

To make a positive life in the midst of what appears to be a negative situation, sniff out and pick up your favorite, familiar memory of a similar experience when you weren't sure about life but managed to survive. A familiar memory of making a positive, successful life in the past settles you right down so you can continue, even in a negative world.

Listen to Life with Your Pet

1. What is your current context in which you're having trouble settling down?

2. Recall a similar, previous circumstance.

3. How did you settle down then? How can you do it again?

Do you check out new situations?

I came home recently to discover a puppy boarding with us. This one was a chocolate Labrador named Hershey. (I'm not making this up.)

My wife told me about the little girl that shares her home with Hershey. She loves her puppy a lot and wasn't so sure about leaving "her Hershey" with someone she didn't know. So, she played 20 Questions with my wife.

She asked questions like, "Will you feed her?"

"Yes," my wife said patiently.

"Will you play with her?"

Again, my wife said, "Yes."

"Can I see where she'll sleep?"

"Of course," my wife said and showed her the kennel.

"She likes treats."

"I'll make sure she gets her treats," my wife told her.

Stooping down to pick up Hershey, the little girl whispered in the puppy's ear, "You'll be fine, Hershey. This lady is nice like me."

With that the little girl was satisfied. She was entrusting someone important to someone else whom she really didn't know and wanted to ensure that everything would be fine. Discovering that it was fine, she could trust her Hershey was in good hands.

Do you ever find yourself in a place of wondering whom to trust, as this little girl did? Like her, you discover yourself in a situation where something or someone dear to you is placed in an unknown circumstance with unknown people.

How do you build trust at times like these?

Play 20 Questions.

Ask everything you care to know. Keep asking until you are positively satisfied. Be specific with your questions. Accept only the right answers.

Trust is essential to making a positive life in this negative world.

Play 20 Questions until you are positive.

Listen to Life with Your Pet

1. When was the last time you played 20 Questions?

2. Did you positively resolve your questions?

3. How can you more positively answer someone's questions to lead them to trust?

Who do you see?

Regularly I come home to discover yet another dog in our home kennel. One day I came home to find a dog barking at me as I walked in the back door. She was barking like she owned the place, was its great protector, and wanted to know who I was and how I got in. I knelt down, held out my open palm, and she sniffed me, barked a couple of more times, and let me pass.

Most of our boarded dogs stay in a kennel, but somehow this dog, Scout, had the run of our home. She barked at me the next day when I came home, protecting her new home. But after that she became accustomed to me as we played, rubbed, and patted. Pretty soon Scout was following me everywhere.

As with Scout and me, getting to know some people takes time, doesn't it? Have you ever thought about what builds that bridge of relationship between you?

For Scout and me, I tolerated her barking at me. Some people bark at you, don't they? It's nothing personal. They bark at everyone. Their spouse, children, coworkers, friends, neighbors. . . . Think of such folks as equal-opportunity barkers. Sometimes getting beyond the barking to knowing the person is a challenge. Maybe they're trying to protect themselves as Scout was. Perhaps they suffered a personal home invasion earlier and aren't sure about trusting others.

I invited Scout to know me on her terms. I opened my palm, showing her I held nothing to hurt her, and allowed her to sniff me. That's a dog's way of getting to know you, identifying you by smell. How do you invite others to identify you? Do you open your life, share some of who you are, and take that first step toward intimacy?

Finally, Scout and I formed a relationship by playing together. When was the last time you played with someone you wanted to know? Or at least took a more playful attitude than the somber, droll, business-as-usual, resume-reciting ritual? Go play and get to know someone.

Why is the creation of new relationships so important? In our relationships we conceive a positive life. We share with another the results of our positive discovery mission on the journey of life. As we share, our results are confirmed, validated, and multiplied, creating a platform from which we launch a positive life not just for ourselves but throughout all of our relationships.

Listen to Life with Your Pet

1. Who is someone you are getting to know?

2. How's that going? Is there barking? An openness? Are you playing together?

3. How can you be more proactive in conceiving a positive life with this person?

What's your perspective?

The hot summer day has cooled off a bit as the sun sets. It's finally pleasant enough for you to walk in your neighborhood. Just a leisurely stroll to stretch your legs.

A growling, barking dog comes running at you, snarling, hair standing up on his back, acting like he hasn't been fed today and your leg is dinner. You instinctively start running, faster than you thought you could. You've got to get away from this "bad dog."

The dog's barking grows fainter as you run so you turn around and see that the dog isn't chasing you. Still growling, barking, and snarling, but not chasing.

So you turn around and head back toward the dog a few steps. You notice that his hind leg is chained and evidently has been for a while because it's cut into his leg, which is bleeding. His ribs stick out like he hasn't been fed in a while. Suddenly the "bad dog" is an abused dog.

Perspective makes all the difference in the world, doesn't it?

Do you understand another's point of view before you judge, criticize, or accuse?

Is it your practice to walk where someone else walks before commenting?

Probably not.

It is far easier for us to pronounce our verdict as judge and jury in an instant than to engage in the time-consuming, often messy task of understanding the context of another's life.

Such expeditious pronouncements make this world negative.

Understanding someone's life situation creates a positive tsunami that transforms all of our relationship tides.

Take the time and energy to consider another person's life context. As you do, you make a positive life in this negative world.

Listen to Life with Your Pet

1. Discovering the abused dog's situation, would you have gone back to feed him?

2. Why? Why not?

3. Sometime today, stop yourself from negatively commenting on someone. Then consider where that person is coming from in life.

If a dog were your teacher, what would you learn?

If a dog were your teacher, you would learn . . .

- When loved ones come home, always run to greet them.

- When it's in your best interest, practice obedience.

- Take naps and stretch before getting up.

If a dog were your teacher, you would learn . . .

- To avoid biting when a simple growl will do.

- On warm days, stop to lie on your back on the grass.

- When you're happy, dance around and wiggle your entire body.

If a dog were your teacher, you would learn . . .

- That no matter how often you're scolded, don't buy into the guilt thing and pout. Run right back and make friends.

- Eat with gusto and enthusiasm. Stop when you've had enough.

- If what you want lies buried, dig until you find it.

And if a dog were your teacher, you would learn . . .

- That when someone is having a bad day, just sit close by and nuzzle them gently.

Listen to Life with Your Pet

1. Which of these lessons have you already learned? Put a check mark beside them.

2. Which of these lessons would you like to learn so you make a positive life?

3. Pick a lesson you've learned and share it with someone today. Pick a lesson you have yet to learn and find someone you believe has learned it. Ask them to help you learn it.

Who is with you now?

A friend shared a story with me about her dog, Sammy. Sammy is a yellow Labrador retriever whom she adopted from one of our litters and evidently is the perfect dog. He's quiet and beautiful. Sammy is energetic on the trail and quiet at camp when my friend rides her horse. He doesn't beg for food and is patient until fed. My friend praises Sammy for being such a great dog, and he wags his tail and smiles at her.

Sammy is her constant companion and one morning accompanied her to the blueberry patch. It's a tranquil setting there, away from traffic noise and beside a gurgling stream. My friend was reveling in the lovely morning and peaceful setting . . . when she realized that she had not spent much time mediating lately. That she had found other things to do than meditate and enjoy the calm solitude of moments with her Creator.

She then looked down at Sammy and realized that just like Sammy, her Creator goes with her everywhere, whether she takes it for granted or not. Like her constant companion, Sammy, her Creator smiles on her whether she's meditating or not . . . all of which drew my friend into a peaceful place within. Far different from the places the world sought to draw her. She wanted to be in that place of positive calm more often.

So standing there in the blueberry patch with Sammy by her side and her Creator all around her, she resolved to invest more of herself and her time, energy, and attention meditating from this peaceful place within.

She says it is how she listens to life and makes a positive life, not just a living, in a negative world.

Listen to Life with Your Pet

1. Do you have a peaceful place within?

2. When do you meditate and experience peace?

3. How can you meditate more often?

How's your attitude?

The talk around town was that Bob, an avid duck hunter, had the best Labrador retriever in the county. However, he refused to take anyone hunting with him to see the dog work. Finally he agreed to let one fellow, Doug, go duck hunting with him. Bob made Doug promise not to tell anyone in town about his dog.

Doug promised and off he went duck hunting with Bob. Doug shot a duck, and the Lab took off to retrieve the downed bird. Instead of swimming, the dog walked on the water to the downed bird, picked it up, and retrieved it, walking on water, back to the hunting blind.

Bob turned to Doug and said, "Now do you understand why I don't want you to tell anyone in town about my dog?"

"Yea, I do," Doug replied. "I wouldn't want anybody to know I owned a dog that couldn't swim."

A dog that can't swim? Or a dog that walks on water? Which do you see in your life?

I guess it depends on your attitude, doesn't it?

After all, you see what you want to see.

Attitude determines what you want to see.

A positive attitude perceives a dog miraculously walking on water.

A negative attitude simply sees a dog that can't swim.

Adjust your attitude to see the dog walk on water.

It's how you listen to life and make a water-walking-dog life, not just a living, in a dog-can't-swim world.

Listen to Life with Your Pet

1. If I asked your family which type of dog you see most often—water walker or nonswimmer—what would they say?

2. If I asked your coworkers the same question, how would they respond?

3. Which attitude do you want to have?

Cats

Penelope our lilac-point Siamese

*"No heaven will not ever heaven be,
unless my cats are there to welcome me."*

Who adopts you?

U ntil then I had never been adopted by a cat. You know that's the way it works with cats. Some people erroneously think they adopt a cat when the exact opposite is true. Sure, you may bring a cat home with you, but that doesn't mean it adopts you. Your cat may just tolerate you, reminding you at least weekly with gifts of mice and voles on your doorstep that "if I so desired, I could take excellent care of myself. I choose to let you feed me."

But sometimes you are blessed, and you invite a cat into your home who actually adopts you and may occasionally act as if she likes you. That's what happened between Samantha and me.

Our relationship started innocently enough. Some would call it coincidence. We thought of it as Providence.

I had taken a new job at a radio station and was preparing to marry my college sweetheart. She had grown up with a cat or two and was particularly fond of a blue-eyed, female seal point Siamese, Tao.

So being the compassionate, intuitive sucker that I am, I called the SPCA shelter in my new town and said something like, "I'm sure no one ever drops off a blue-eyed, female seal point Siamese cat, but if someone does in the next few weeks, would you give me a call?"

The silence was finally broken by, "How did you know?"

"How did I know what?" I said.

"We found a blue-eyed, female seal point Siamese cat in our drop-off box this morning."

"Oh," I said. "I'll be right over."

And that's how Samantha adopted me. At first she tolerated me. Remember, I had never been adopted by a cat. I didn't know how to hold, pet, feed, or sleep with one. I didn't know what was wrong with her when she cried all night for a mate, how to take her to the vet to get rid of the plumbing problem that made her cry all night. In fact, I knew nothing about cats.

But Samantha was patient.

She taught me which food she preferred by scattering the cheap stuff all over the kitchen and scarfing down the expensive variety.

She helped me understand when the litter box required cleaning by squatting and going in the corner.

She prepared me for married life by stretching out and taking up two-thirds of the bed each night and snoring.

Once I satisfactorily completed Samantha's adoption orientation program, she decided to keep me. That made my wife happy since Samantha was her wedding gift.

Patient preparation for life is such a wonderful gift, isn't it?

You know it when you receive it from others.

You wish you had given more of it to others.

I guess that's why Samantha and I regarded our relationship as more Providence than coincidence. Patience comes only from Providence.

Why does it sometimes hurt so badly?

Samantha was the first cat to adopt me. I felt privileged. She knew I was. We were about as close as a cat and her adoptee could be. My wife still tells the story of waking up in the mornings when we were newlyweds, and there was Samantha, under the covers, between us, snuggled up next to me with her head on my pillow. Remember now, Samantha was my wedding gift to my wife. A wedding gift who slept between us.

This close relationship made it all the more difficult when I could no longer ignore Samantha's labored breathing. I asked my wife what we should do.

"Take her to the vet," she said.

Tests were taken and the vet's grim face told the story.

"I'm so sorry," she said. "Samantha has cancer. Looks like it started in her mammary glands, and now it's in her lungs and growing. It will only get worse."

Surgery was an option, she told us. I said, "Please do everything you can."

Following surgery, she said, "I did the best I could, but it's everywhere."

Then those fateful words, "You may want to end her suffering soon and put her to sleep."

It was a long, silent trip as Sam, my wife, and I went home, "the decision" choking us like a stubborn hairball.

One day Samantha made it easier on me. She spent most of her time

---

asleep from the medicine. But this day she found me and staggered into my leg, rubbing on me the best she could—her way of asking, "Pick me up."

I did. She lay limp in my arms . . . until she raised her head a bit, closed her eyes, smiled ever so slightly, and purred. One quick, short burst of purr. As if to say, "I'll be OK."

We left Samantha with the vet the next morning. I couldn't drive home, unable to see through the tears which just would not stop.

"Why does it hurt so badly?" I asked myself. "She was just a cat."

Then I remembered that last burst of purr and corrected myself.

She was not just a cat, I thought, smiling ever so slightly.

She was my cat. She adopted me.

Listen to Life with Your Pet

1. In your life experiences who has adopted you?

2. How are you better for the shared life?

3. Who can you adopt and give a positive life?

Who listens to you?

My wife was only 15 years old when her mom died. Even after all of these years of marriage, I still can't fully imagine how painful that must have been—a teenage girl who should be enjoying the excitement of a driving permit, a first date and kiss, and high school forced to say good-bye to her mom.

I remember asking my wife one day, "How did you make it through?"

That's when she began to tell me stories about Tao, the female seal point Siamese cat that prompted me to search for Samantha, and Magnolia who suffered through the humiliation of being a 20-pound, pink-nosed male tabby whose owners called him "Maggie."

Tao was your typical Siamese—persnickety and snitty, tolerating people because she chose to.

Maggie constantly fought with raccoons and other neighborhood cats, a neurotic symptom from the trauma of living with his name.

And yet Tao and Maggie somehow knew and therefore changed personalities when with my wife. "They always knew when to curl up next to me as I lay crying on my bed," she says. "They listened without interrupting me, smiling like they understood." She credits Tao and Maggie with helping her make it through the grief.

Listening without interrupting is a rare and joyous gift, isn't it?

Receiving an understanding smile is an uncommon and delightful present, isn't it?

Such gifts and presents are an integral part of your positive life. As you conceive the positive in the negative world, have you noticed that as you give them away, they multiply? They brighten someone's day. They lighten another's burden.

Listen without interrupting.

Offer an understanding smile.

You conceive a positive life as you do.

Listen to Life with Your Pet

1. Who listens to you without interrupting? How does such listening make you more positive?

2. Who offers you an understanding smile? How does that simple smile make you more positive?

3. Who will you listen to without interrupting? Who will you give an understanding smile?

What do you see?

I painted our kitchen as a birthday present for my wife. Yes, it was a present because she wanted the colors changed, and I'm a good painter.

We have a large bay window there overlooking the front part of our farm. Painting around that window gave me a chance to enjoy our incredible view of the Appalachian Mountains. Plus I could watch one of our cats, Maybelle.

I rescued Maybelle from a four-year-old boy whose idea of fun was to put her in a cooler, shut the top, go play for a while, and come back to check on her. After watching him do this for the better part of an hour, I said to his mom, "You don't really want that cat, do you?" Sixty seconds later Maybelle was in my car, on the way home.

Maybelle enjoyed a wonderful life on our farm. She could catch mice in the hay barn. She could dig up voles in the yard. And she could terrorize birds just by walking by.

So as I painted, I put down my brush and watched her antics. One day she walked up to a dogwood tree. At first she put her front paws on it and stretched. Then she looked up the tree, sized it up, and turned her head to the side as if to ask, "What's up there?"

Curiosity got the best of her, and she climbed up the tree. She went up as far as she safely could, pretty close to the top, where the branches grew too small to support her. So here she was, near the top of the tree when she stretched out her neck and started looking around, shifting her weight to get a 360-degree view. Then satisfied, she climbed back down.

Making your life positive in this negative world has to include Maybelle's curiosity. A sense of wonderment of "What's up there?" or no reason for doing something other than "just because."

Be like Maybelle. Let curiosity be your guide as you make a positive life, not just a living today.

Listen to Life with Your Pet

1.   Do you take the time to be curious? To pursue something of interest, even a passing interest, "just because"? Why? Why not?

2.   How is your sense of awe with the world around you?

3.   When will you be curious today?

Are you purring?

I sat, relaxing with the newspaper, enjoying some quiet time. It was a beautiful fall morning, so cool and crisp that I opened a window. Suddenly a bird started making all kinds of loud noises just outside the window. Not singing noises, but "Danger Will Robinson!" noises. At first I ignored it, but it continued loudly. Finally, I got up to investigate.

As I stepped out on the porch, I saw the bird—a baby mockingbird—perched in the Japanese maple tree, squawking at Maybelle the curious cat, who reclined on the porch in a most regal manner, gazing off across her horse pastures.

The baby mockingbird who bothered me was not bothering Maybelle at all. She saw me, sauntered over, and rubbed herself against my legs, granting me permission to pet her.

So I stooped down for a couple of minutes and petted her. She purred. All the while, this baby bird still screamed at us. Maybelle just did not mind. She ignored the bird and focused on letting me pet her.

Someone or something in life is always squawking at you, isn't it?

At times, do you seem to hear more squawkers than usual? Like they conspired against you to ruin your day? Everyone wants everything from you right now? As if they know you're trying your best to make a positive life and want to drag you down into the negativity?

In such times, relax like Maybelle. Avoid getting upset. Just ignore the squawkers. They have no more power or influence in your life than you give them.

Instead, find someone who's positive. Go rub elbows with them and purr.

That's how you can listen to life and make a positive life, not just a living, in a negative world.

Listen to Life with Your Pet

1. Who is your most recent squawker?

2. How did you react?

3. Next time, how will you be more like Maybelle?

Who do you help?

For the first time in our married lives we found ourselves catless.

A most unique and tragic place for us.

Maybelle left us, dying in my wife's arms late one night. Norman followed soon after. I'll always believe he grieved himself to death, missing Maybelle. Life just wasn't right.

No one to weave between my legs as I tried to grab my laptop and coffee carafe and get out of the car.

No one to chase falling leaves in the autumn.

No one to leave mouse-carcass presents on the back porch.

Life just wasn't right . . . until the New Guy moved in. His previous owners said he didn't get along with their other cat who adopted them first so he had to go. "Something is just wrong with this cat," their daughter told ours. "He's stupid."

Oh boy, I thought, knowing that all cats carry within them certain neuroses.

So New Guy moved in. His previous owners called him Scout. Thinking he needed a new name for a new life, my wife suggested we call him Boo Radley.

Scout / New Guy / Boo Radley took to his new life as if he were a predestination-believing, once-saved-always-saved Presbyterian-Baptist. "This is where I have belonged since birth," his prance around the farm suggested. He adopted us immediately.

Boo and I first became acquainted as I planted annual flowers one Saturday morning. It was already hot enough to fry an egg on my bald head, and here came Boo Radley, meowing his "Good morning!" as he sauntered over.

Immediately he started digging up a marigold I had just sunk into the ground, pulling up the roots and all. I'm sure I yelled something at him. Probably not something I'm proud to repeat here, but I'll blame it on the heat and my sweating bald head.

He scampered away, and I thought that was the end of that. But no, here he came again, slinking back over, meowing ever so softly, as if to say, "Sorry about that."

"OK, me, too," I said. "Now if you're going to help, you have to do something useful like help me dig the holes."

With that, I plunged my spade into the ground and dug up some dirt. The next thing I knew, Boo Radley walked over to the hole I just dug, stuck his paw into it, and began digging. Fast and furious, too. Then he stopped, looked up, and said, "Meow?"

Naturally since then Boo and I are best of friends. I guess it was pre-destined that we save each other.

Listen to Life with Your Pet

1. When have you received a new start?

2. Do you have that feeling of "This is where I have belonged since birth"? Why? Why not?

3. Who have you given a second chance to make a positive life with you?

Do you have a special power?

A mother who listens to life through www.ListentoLife.org shared a story of how her six-year-old son walked up to her one day and said, "Mommy, I have a special power!"

"Oh really," she said. "What kind of special power do you have?"

And the little boy said, "I can talk to animals and they understand me."

Well, of course, the mother thought, *Oh great! He's another Dr. Doolittle. I'll have to spend tens of thousands of dollars on therapy.*

Instead she said to him, "Really? Well, how do you know you have this special power?"

And he said, "Because I tell our cat, 'I love you,' and she licks my face."

That really is a special power, isn't it? The special power of love.

We can tell each other, "I love you" and give each other love back. As we do, we conceive a positive life with another that grows exponentially across time and space.

Will you perceive the day coming when the world defines power not as money or military strength but as love?

Will you conceive of how your life will positively grow and improve sharing this special power of love?

Will you believe what a wonderful world this will be as more of us start using our special power of love?

Will you achieve a positive transformation of your part of the world by unleashing this special power of love?

Will you receive the special power of love as you positively give it away?

Tell someone "I love you!" as you listen to life and make a positive life, not just a living, in a negative world today.

Listen to Life with Your Pet

1. Recall someone who recently shared their special power of love with you.

2. Relive that experience.

3. Who will you share your special power of love with today?

Do all cats go to heaven, too?

Here are some letters cats might write to God:

- "Dear God, when we get to heaven, can we scratch on your sofa? Or is it the same spray water bottle treatment?"

- "Dear God, if a cat yowls his head off in the middle of a forest and no human hears him, does he still get yelled at?"

- "Dear God, is it true there's an eternal supply of catnip in heaven?"

- "Dear God, will I hark up hair balls in heaven? If I do, will I still have to make those embarrassing coughing sounds in that funny position?"

- "Dear God, if heaven is truly heaven, then the litter box is clean eternally, right?"

- "Dear God, if you let me into heaven, I'll adopt you."

- "Dear God, please tell me that dogs don't get into heaven. Certainly not all of them, correct?"

- "Dear God, if all the dogs really do get in, please tell me they have to stay outside."

Listen to Life with Your Pet

1. How do you describe heaven?

2. How does it resemble your positive life now?

3. Do all cats go to heaven, too?

What gets your motor running?

A mother who listens to life through our Web site at www.ListentoLife.org emailed me with the story about the time she and her three-year-old son played with their cat, Smokey. Smokey purred loudly, enjoying all of the attention and was obviously happy.

The mother said, "Listen to Smokey's motor running."

Her son quickly said in that sweet three-year-old language, "That not her motor running. That love in her heart!"

Even though her son is much older now, every time she hears a cat purr, she remembers that they have love in their hearts.

If you want to make a positive life, not just a living, in this negative world, get your motor running with love in your heart.

Listen to Life with Your Pet

1. Does your heart-motor run on love?

2. Do the people around you—at home, work, and in the neighborhood—know?

3. How can they tell? How do you purr?

What's heaven like?

A cat dies and goes to heaven. God meets her and says, "You've been a good cat all of these years. Anything you desire is yours. All you have to do is ask."

So the cat says, "Well, I lived all my life with a poor family on a farm and had to sleep on hardwood floors."

God says, "Say no more," and instantly a fluffy pillow appears.

A few days later six mice die and they go to heaven. God greets them at the gate with the same offer the cat received. And the mice said, "All our lives we've had to run from being chased. If we could only have a pair of roller skates, we wouldn't have to run anymore."

God says, "Say no more," and instantly each mouse is fitted with a pair of tiny roller skates.

About a week later God decides to check and see how the cat is doing. She's sound asleep on her new pillow. God gently wakes her and asks, "How are you doing?"

The cat says, "Oh, I've never been happier in my life. And those meals on wheels you're sending over are the best."

So what's your heaven like?

Imagine your positive life today and ask for it!

Listen to Life with Your Pet

1. What is heaven to you?

2. What do you lack here that you hope to have there?

3. "How are you doing?"

Horses

My daughter with Leo

*"A dog may be a person's best friend,
but a horse made history."*

Do you lie around horses?

I'll forever remember the first time I rode a horse.

I wanted to ride a horse so much that I lied to get on it.

My best friend's grandfather owned a farm and had horses. Before we arrived, my friend coached me, "Now Granddaddy will ask you if you've ever ridden a horse before. You tell him yes, or else he'll want to ride with us and might not let us go."

Just as my friend predicted, as we prepared to go riding, his grandfather said, "So Joey, have you ever ridden a horse before?"

My friend looked at me and I looked at him. It was one of those defining moments of truth or dare. I conjured up a quick memory of sitting on a pony at the county fair, those ponies that walk in a circle because they're all tied together. I said, "Yes sir, I have."

Sizing me up, he said, "Well good, you boys should have some fun then."

My friend and I breathed a sigh of relief. We were free!

They brought my horse over to me, and he was absolutely the biggest creature I had ever stood next to. And I thought, *This is no pony at the county fair.*

After Gargantuan, my horse, was saddled, my friend came over to give me a leg up on the massive beast. "Grab the horn," he whispered. "Put your left foot in this stirrup and throw yourself up on top."

So I did and discovered that Gargantuan was even taller than I thought. I swung up and landed across the saddle, not in it. I squirmed around like an upside-down turtle, legs kicking and flaying, praying I could regain my balance on an air molecule and sit down. My friend grabbed my right leg, threw it over, and I sat up, triumphant and confident. The grandfather stared at me with an amusing smile.

"The horse I rode before was shorter," I said.

He just kept smiling. He knew. And I knew he knew. I lied.

I realized then that I didn't have a clue about what to do next. I grabbed the saddle horn with all the intensity and hope of a drowning man latching onto a life preserver, thinking this was my only salvation. My friend threw the reins up to me. I seized them, and began pulling back to keep Gargantuan from taking off on me. Visions of *Bonanza's* Little Joe on a runaway horse galloped through my mind.

The horse took my cue and began backing up. That sent me into a modified panic, looking around for the emergency brake.

"Well," the grandfather said, "if he's ridden a horse before, I guess he knows if you pull back on the reins, the horse backs up."

I relaxed the reins and the horse stood still.

Now Gargantuan joined the grandfather in knowing that I lied.

I don't know who had more fun that day, the horse or me. You see, I obviously didn't have a clue about how to ride a horse, which means Gargantuan went where he wanted to go when he wanted to go. He ignored my frequent "Whoa!" He ate grass as he pleased. He galloped at will. He had his way with me. But I loved every moment of it because I was riding a horse just like the Lone Ranger and Gene Autry and Jim West and, most of all, John Wayne.

Since that first experience, I've discovered that I'm not the only one who lies about horses. In fact, there are more of us who lie about horses than tell the truth. Once I bought a horse from a fellow who, when I asked him if anything was wrong with the horse, looked me straight in the eye and said, "Nope."

The horse was blind in one eye.

Despite all the lies, there are some good things to be said about horses and the people who have them. For instance, I bought our daughters their own horses. They grew up riding and caring for them. A friend asked me why I bought my daughters horses. I told him, "I'd rather my daughters smell like hay and horse manure on Friday night than some boy's cologne."

That worked out just fine until they turned 16 and traded horses for horsepower. But by that time they had learned that responsibility jogs alongside freedom. That while we're free to lie if we choose, we still have to be responsible for the outcomes. Sure, they could lie about cooling down their horses after riding to get to supper a little faster, but the next day when their horses didn't feel well enough to ride, they lived with the consequences. Of course, they could tell their mom, "Yes ma'am, I cleaned the stalls" when they didn't really do a good job; but when Mom found out the truth, not only did the stalls get cleaned but a privilege was lost as well.

And yes, they even had the audacity to lie when I asked, "So has your friend ever ridden a horse before?" As they walked away, I could only hope they would have as good a time as I did that first day and learn that most valuable lesson:

When you think no one knows you're lying, they really do.

Even the horses.

Are you a prisoner?

My wife boards horses for people who enjoy just riding. She received some new horses to board that came from South Dakota. The farm where they stayed before coming to us was set up differently than ours. The horses were in much smaller areas.

One of the horses was especially large and really didn't enjoy the small space he was in previously. His temperament was rather cranky. He picked on the other three horses, biting their tails and nipping their necks. He crowded them away from the water trough. It was easy to assume he had a bad attitude.

The interesting thing to me was watching him gently begin to explore our larger pasture; and as he did, his attitude improved. At first he stood basically in one spot all day, just as he had in South Dakota. In his mind he was still enclosed in a small space. Never mind he had five acres of pasture to enjoy. He didn't move. He was still a mental prisoner.

Then one day, for some reason he took a few steps toward the open pasture. He began walking a square which I suppose was a little larger than his previous paddock. After a day of walking this expanded area, he broadened his horizons just a bit more and went farther. He even put his head down and began to eat the grass in his new area.

The next day he stood at the edge of his newly discovered area and looked long and hard across the rolling pasture. In an act of courage and burst of inspiration, he took off galloping across the field, kicking up his hooves and throwing his head as if to say, "I'm free! I'm free!" He was no longer an inmate of the small paddock in his mind.

Only gradually did this horse's mental picture of where he could spend the day expand to include all the pasture. As long as he chose to remain a prisoner in his mind, he would be. And yet he held the key to the lock in his perception the entire time.

Once he discovered the entire pasture, he never stood in just one small spot again.

Listen to Life with Your Pet

1. What mental prison do you choose to stay in? How are you trapping yourself in a small area of life?

2. What does your larger life and freedom look like?

3. What will you do today to expand gradually your area and pick the lock of your mind to live positive?

Do you go with the herd?

A six-year-old friend of mine got excited when she discovered that I live with horses on our farm. She asked our horses' names and wanted to know what they looked like. I said, "Do you like horses?"

"Yes, I do," she said. "I went to horse camp last summer."

"You did?" I said. "Was it fun?"

"You betcha," she said. "The teacher told me that it's hard to ride ponies. They're hard to handle. But they weren't hard for me. I thought they were easy."

"Why were they easy for you?" I said.

"I didn't believe the teacher. I just got on and rode," she said.

Sounds like a great way to live positive to me, don't you think?

How many times do you let someone else tell you that something you want to do is hard, or impossible, or a real challenge? And then you believe them? Which of course makes the task hard, impossible, and a real challenge?

Think back to a recent team meeting for work. Ideas were passing around the table. All of you were plucking the best ones and creating a beautiful plan to boost sales or increase profits or meet your customers' needs in new and exciting ways. Just then someone said something like, "Definitely won't work," or "That'll be too hard," or "It's impossible." All the air of enthusiastic excitement and limitless possibilities went out of the room, didn't it?

Or maybe you and your family were discussing a dream vacation. You talked about the fun of taking a trip together to some place really special. Each of you, even the children, talked about taking on a part-time job to help pay for it. Just then, one family member said, "This is just too expensive. There's no way we can pay for this." Everyone's shoulders slumped in discouragement.

I call such persons "Eeyores," after the Winnie the Pooh character. Their constant refrain is, "It'll never work."

If you want to live positive like my six-year-old friend, limit the amount of power you give to Eeyores. Avoid letting them shape your attitude. Distance yourself from their influence.

You see, the majority—the herd—is usually wrong about what's impossible or what won't work. I mean, if it were easy, everyone would be doing it, right?

Choose to live positive and work positive by not herding with the Eeyores.

Listen to Life with Your Pet

1. Recall a recent encounter with an Eeyore.

2. How did you react?

3. Reflecting back on your experience and this story, how would you choose to react now?

Do all horses go to heaven, also?

If horses could write letters to God, here is what I bet they would say:

- "When we get to heaven, can we graze where we want to? I mean, heaven doesn't have fences, does it?"

- "If a horse neighs his head off in the pasture and no human hears him, is he still a bad horse?"

- "I heard you get a rubdown every day in heaven. Is that right?"

- "Does it rain in heaven? And do we have to stand out in it?"

- "Are there jockey races in heaven? And do we get to bet on them?"

- "If there are jockey races in heaven, can we ride them? And can we use those whips?"

- "Is it true that all of the feed is sweet up there?"

- "If I still crib in heaven, I don't have to wear a collar, do I? And I get to stay because all horses go to heaven, right?"

Listen to Life with Your Pet

1. What would your horse describe as heavenly?

2. How do you describe heaven?

3. How are you and your horse enjoying heaven together now?

Is your pasture greener?

My wife boards horses on our farm, our horses and those belonging to other people who enjoy getting out of the city and riding along beautiful trails. She loves those horses. Her passion in life is caring for animals, and she really enjoys it every day.

She rotates the horses from one pasture to another so they have enough grass to graze. Our part of the world had wonderful spring rains one year which meant that the grass grew beautifully, filling the pastures abundantly.

One morning she moved the horses from one pasture into another. I watched as she took them from the pasture where they had grazed the grass down pretty low into this new pasture where the grass was new and tall. It literally shone in the morning sun, kind of an electric green; the dew glistening while it clung to the newborn grass.

As the horses entered the new pasture one by one, their ears perked up, and their pace quickened. I imagined their nickering conversations as something like:

"Oh boy! Look at this delicious buffet!"

"Can you believe this? This can't be true!"

"Do you know how long I've been staring at this pasture, drooling over it?"

They put their heads down and started eating and didn't pick them up until hours later when they were full.

Life is filled with such goodness not just for those horses but for you as well. You have a goodness in life, kind of like the green pasture for the horses.

Yes, I know. Life is heavy and hard to take sometimes. And you can stay in that brown pasture as long as you choose.

Life is also good sometimes. In fact, occasionally it's great!

Which pasture do you prefer?

Even if life is heavy and hard to take today, change pastures. Move over to where the grass is greener.

Then put your head down and eat until you're full of a positive life.

Listen to Life with Your Pet

1. When did you find yourself recently in a greener pasture?

2. What was your reaction on finding it?

3. How can you get back there when you're in a brown pasture?

Do you sleep soundly?

A t one time my office was on our farm, overlooking our horse pastures. I enjoyed looking out over the pastures between phone appointments and during breaks from writing and recording. It's an idyllic view.

One day I noticed a couple of our horses, Sugar and Seeker, lying on the ground, stretched out flat. It's unusual to see them like that. Usually they sit up and don't lie flat. I looked more closely out of concern, thinking that something had gone wrong.

Then I saw our third horse, Leo, standing nearby, almost at attention. He looked around the area at anything that moved. He guarded his two pasture mates while they slept soundly.

I then understood why Sugar and Seeker could sleep lying completely flat on the ground: Leo guarded them against danger.

I realized as I listened to my life in that moment that I am guarded in life, too. You are, also.

In fact, at times, you and I may be unaware of how we're guarded.

Remember that stoplight that caught you when you were in a hurry to get to your next appointment? What if your stopping prevented you from being in an accident at the next intersection?

How about that person who called out to you when you dropped a $20 bill from your purse going into the pharmacy? That was your prescription money for the month, wasn't it?

Was it just coincidence that the man in line behind you at the grocery store bought your infant's formula when your debit card wouldn't work because the bank had not yet credited your payroll check?

Yes, you are guarded just as Leo stood over Sugar and Seeker. Sure, bad things still happen to you. Life is not perfect. But you can sleep soundly, knowing you are not alone.

So don't worry so much. Listen to your life and make a positive life, not just a living, in a negative world.

Listen to Life with Your Pet

1. Relive a recent occasion when you were delayed or otherwise inconvenienced. How could that situation have played out were it not for the delay?

2. Remember a life experience when you knew you were guarded.

3. Who can you help guard today?

What do you take for granted?

One beautiful fall day our family took a couple of our horses to an outdoor festival to help a group raise money to put a new roof on their facility. Moms and dads gave a donation, and in exchange their child got to ride one of our horses.

We led the horses around in a large circle so basically the children just sat on the horse. We ride Western saddle so most of the kids had a death grip on the horn while we walked. They just weren't accustomed to riding.

I watched every one of those children closely. Walking up to the horse, their eyes grew large and wide open. Then just as soon as they were seated, every single one of them started smiling, and their eyes lit up, dancing and twinkling like so many stars on a clear, dark night.

When they got settled and comfortable, they smiled. That was my cue to start walking the horse. As I walked them around, I talked to the children. I asked them, "Have you ever ridden a horse before?" and "Do you like horses?" or "This horse's name is Leo. What's your name?" One little girl enjoyed several rides that day. Now she takes riding lessons at least once a week.

As I looked up and down the line of excited children who literally shook with excitement, I thought: *Our family can ride these horses any day of the week we choose. These kids can't. They consider a thrill of a lifetime what we take for granted.*

Enjoy all of your positive life that you're making. Take nothing for granted.

Listen to Life with Your Pet

1. What do you take for granted that is a real positive in your life?

2. What do you do or can do that others can't but want to?

3. How can you share this positive with others, thereby increasing your enjoyment?

Do you know how much you're loved?

My wife has a registered quarter horse that she absolutely loves. Seeker is a tall and lean sorrel mare with a sweet disposition. She and my wife do well together. My wife is careful about whom she lets work on her horse when it's time for the vet or the farrier.

I was at the horse barn with her when the farrier showed up to shoe her horse. I knew he must be great at what he does or he wouldn't be at our farm. So I watched him closely to see why he's the best.

Here's what I noticed. He took his time with Seeker, getting to know her and giving her an opportunity to know him. When the time seemed right, he didn't just pick up any horseshoe out of his rack and throw it on her hoof. Instead, he carefully measured her hoof, took the shoe to the anvil and banged it into shape, measured it again against her hoof, banged it some more, took it over to the grinder, smoothed off some rough edges, then measured it some more.

He patiently worked that shoe into the just-right shape for Seeker's hoof until finally, when he was satisfied that it fit perfectly, he nailed it in place. He didn't put it on her until he was satisfied with the fit.

He finished up by trimming off the ends of the nails. Then he sealed the hoof.

Now do you understand why my wife has him as her farrier? He gives that same fine attention to detail to every horse he shoes.

Like my wife's farrier, life gives you that same fine attention to detail.

Life works with you until the circumstances in your life fit perfectly. Your satisfaction with your life fit is important. Daily new and positive experiences seal your life with unconditional love.

Now do you understand how much you're loved?

Listen to Life with Your Pet

1.   What's happened in your life recently that fit you just right?

2.   How does that event remind you how much you're loved?

3.   When do you expect that to happen again?

When the seasons change, what do you wear?

W hen the seasons change, it's hard to know what to wear sometimes, isn't it? One day it's warm outside, and the next it's really cool.

You ask yourself, "Do I wear a sweater?" or "Am I going to need a jacket?"

As fall transitioned into winter one year, I noticed that our horses were starting to get their winter coats. Their sleek, summertime bodies responded to the changing temperatures with more and longer hair. Our dogs' fur was thickening up. Even our cats were growing an extra layer.

Like our pets I put on something extra—a jacket a few mornings and evenings. That's when I decided it was time to change out the clothes in my closet, to move the short-sleeved shirts out and bring down the long-sleeved shirts from the attic. No more silk Hawaiian shirts. Break out the cotton flannel ones.

As I exchanged my clothes, I saw some short-sleeved shirts that I didn't wear that year. Maybe they were a little faded or out of style or just not one of my favorites. I mean, how many shirts can a guy wear?

So I decided to separate all of the shirts I didn't wear and any slacks, too, and create a different pile. I mean, if I didn't wear them this year, what makes me think I'll wear them next year? I didn't move them into attic storage.

Instead, I gave them to a local clothes closet that provides clothing to persons whose homes burned in a fire, or who were laid off from their jobs, or some other situation that created a need.

When you live positive, you discover that yes, you transform your thoughts, behaviors, and beliefs to enjoy your positive life; but you also realize that you receive your positive life. You see that what goes around, comes around. That others helped you along the way and you want to do the same.

Gratitude for receiving causes you to give.

Giving attracts receiving.

Your positive life is yours to make in this negative world.

Listen to Life with Your Pet

1. Just as our horses grow and shed their winter coats, what can you grow and shed in your positive life?

2. What clothes can you give away as the seasons change this year?

3. Look in your closet and decide which clothes you're keeping and which you're not wearing that someone else would enjoy.

Are you blessed only to discover it much later?

Our pets are really important to us. My family and I live on a horse farm. I work for my wife on the farm. I'm in charge of maintenance, which basically means I fix stuff when it breaks.

The fences around the horse pastures are one of the things commonly broken. Most of the time the culprits are deer. Some of these deer are aerial acrobats, jumping high in the air from a flat-out run and landing gracefully on the other side. However, some deer—evidently quite a few—jump like me. They have the best of intentions but miss and don't make it over the boards. Instead they break them.

Well, one morning I discovered that more than just boards were broken. Several posts were knocked down as well. The strand of electric wire around the fence stayed up but barely. In fact, the fence was so messed up that had the horses realized it, they could have gotten out. I had no idea the fence was broken during the night. If I had, we would have moved the horses to another pasture.

As some of my daughter's friends and I repaired the posts and boards, I was grateful that none of the horses escaped. During the night I was blessed and didn't even know it.

Do you ever find yourself where I was? Blessed and not even knowing it?

As I coach people to live positive, one of the keys to success is to remember these life experiences when you were blessed and didn't even know it. To recall regularly occasions in which you watched resources beyond your control or even influence converge to your positive advantage.

As you recall such positive life experiences, you begin to believe that you will make a positive life even in a negative world.

Listen to Life with Your Pet

1. Recall a time in your life when you knew you experienced more than you originally realized.

2. How did this positive event occur?

3. How did it transform your beliefs about your positive life?

Who do you answer to?

Living on a horse farm means my wife and I enjoy taking care of our pets but also the farm. One morning I left our home and headed down our quarter-mile-long driveway toward the highway and noticed that some of our fencing was down. I suppose it was those pesky deer again.

I stopped, got out of the car, looked at the fence, and propped it back up the best I could. I was on my way to an appointment and didn't have time to change clothes and fix it. However, I knew I had to come back and fix it pretty quickly. And I did, wondering how long it had been that way.

The next day I saw several friends who said something to me like, "Yea, I saw your fence down and started to call you and tell you, but I thought you probably knew it." The fact is I didn't.

As with fences, so it is with life. Other people see situations in your life and sometimes before you do. I guess it's another excellent example of the forest and trees. You can't see one because you're looking at the other.

That's why I find it so important as I listen to life and make a positive life, not just a living, in a negative world to have people in my life who check in with me, who hold me accountable for what's going on and how I'm dealing with it.

Now understand that I don't ask just anyone to assist me in being surgically honest with myself. These people are friends who have a strong sense of themselves—their strengths and weaknesses. These friends have manageable egos that rarely get in the way of our relationship. Humility and honesty are two of their core values. Also, they care enough about me to invest in me to a level of understanding and accountability. They want what's best for me.

One of the keys to success for you in making a positive life is to choose carefully friends who will tell you when your fence is down. These are the folks with whom you conceive a positive life, combining your unique gifts and sensibilities to create a positive synergy that is mutually beneficial. They care enough to be honest with you. They hold you accountable.

Discover such friends as you listen to your life and make a positive life, not just a living.

Listen to Life with Your Pet

1. Name one person who cares enough about you to let you know when something is not quite right in your life.

2. Does this person have the qualities of honesty, humility, compassion, and understanding? If so, how have you seen these displayed?

3. When will you ask this person to be a partner in creating your positive life?

What do you dread?

I made a mistake putting up a fencepost for a gate around one of our pastures.

I didn't measure for my gate properly before I planted the posts for it.

Of course I realized this when I brought the gate home and tried to hang it. It just didn't quite reach. The whole purpose of the gate is to close and keep the horses in. It didn't work.

I got upset with myself when I discovered what I'd done. You see, I put some cement around the post. Digging up chunks of cement isn't exactly my favorite pastime. OK, I hate doing it.

So rather than just go ahead and dig up and move the post, I put it off. I procrastinated.

Amazingly I found all of these other jobs to do. All of a sudden, they appeared out of nowhere. Every single one of these new jobs was preferable to the post job.

The longer I procrastinated moving the post, the more I dreaded doing it until after a while, in my mind at least, you'd have thought I was moving a mountain.

One weekend I decided that the day had come when I had to get over myself and just move that post. I brought out my tools and started digging. Amazingly, the job was far easier than my imagination made it out to be. I finished in about an hour.

Making a positive life doesn't mean that you ignore the negative experiences. If you do like I did with my post mistake, you discover that they don't go away. Negative experiences happen to all of us.

Amazingly the more we dwell on the negativity, the larger it grows.

The same is true about positivity. Dwell on it and it grows.

Not all of your efforts produce positive results. So what do you do with them?

I learned to more carefully measure when putting up gate posts. To keep taking measurements up until the last shovel of cement goes in the hole to ensure accuracy.

My negative experience became a positive one. Every gate post I put up since that experience works well.

So was it really a negative experience? Or a pathway to a lifetime of positive ones?

Soon you will make a mistake and face something you dread doing to correct it. Just take a deep breath, find the positive lesson, and fix it. It's a lot easier than you think!

Listen to Life with Your Pet

1. What mistake have you made lately?

2. How did you think and feel about correcting it?

3. Write down what you learned and how you have benefited from that experience.

Do you have the "sit down and quits"?

Do you ever try to do something alone and discover that you can't?

You push on the problem, or kick the chaos, or deny the dilemma; and no matter what you do, you just can't budge it?

You can't pull the load alone. So you just sit down and quit.

The story is told of a man driving a wagon pulled by a mule named Jim. When everyone got on the wagon, the driver yelled, "Giddyup, Jim. Giddyup, Sue. Giddyup, Sam. Giddyup, John. Giddyup, Joe."

As the wagon started to move, one of the passengers was rather mystified by the wagon master calling all of those names. He said, "When Jim is the one and only mule you have there, why do you call the other names?"

And the owner said, "If Jim knew he was the only one pulling this wagon, he'd never budge an inch."

The "sit down and quits" are pervasive today. You aren't the only one tempted to give up on a positive life when it seems that the negative world is taking over.

But you might feel like you're the only one.

That is because you're like Jim should he think he's the only one pulling the wagon. It seems the whole load is yours and yours alone.

The reality is that like Jim, you really don't know what you can do until you try. You are capable of limitless positivity in life. Your perceiving your life as positive creates a lot more horsepower for dealing with life than you imagine.

Also, you're not really pulling that life load alone. Generations have come before you, each one tempted never to budge an inch. And yet each one accomplishing far more than any could ever imagine.

You will as well. Pull hard and positively perceive your life so you can make a positive life, not just a living today, even in a negative world.

Listen to Life with Your Pet

1. When was the last time you felt alone in pulling against a heavy life load?

2. Did you "sit down and quit"? Or keep pulling?

3. What was your result? How did it determine how you live your positive life?

Do you see in the dark?

My wife was out of town for an overnight trip with the girls. I was feeding some of our horses. It was an extremely dark night, cloudy with no starlight.

This group of horses is fed outside, not in the barn, in pails on the ground. Sometimes they play with their pails and roll them around the pasture. So here I am, looking for black pails on the ground to pour the feed into on an extremely dark night.

I searched all over the usual spots where the pails are. Nothing.

If you've ever fed horses, you know that from the second they see or hear you filling the buckets, you are the center of attention. And from the nanosecond you enter that gate carrying those buckets, you are not alone. The horses are beside you. The more aggressive like Leo try to stick their head into a bucket, hoping to steal a mouthful. You would think they had not been fed in a week.

So here I am, on a dark night looking for black pails on the ground in which to pour feed, being bumped by impatient horses intent on eating right now. I'm sure it was a comical scene, hilarious even. But I just knew one of them was going to step on my foot.

Finally I thought, *Instead of stumbling around the pasture with horses chasing you for feed, let the horses show you where the pails are.*

So I took another step into the pasture in what I hoped was the direction of the pails, spoke to the horses and told them to "go on," and watched as they went and stood in various places around the pasture. I walked up to each one and discovered a black pail on the ground in front of them, poured in the feed, and moved on to the next one.

While I couldn't see the black pails on the ground on a dark night, the horses could see them. I let the horses guide me.

Do you ever find yourself stumbling around in the darkness of your life for something?

And it seems as if the more you look for it, the harder it is to find?

Then as you stumble around, it gets even harder to find it because others are bumping you, trying to steal some of what you do have?

Trust me. I know. It's not easy to make a positive life in this negative world.

However it is simple. Be still.

There's Someone who sees what you can't in your darkness and will lead you to where you want to be.

Listen to Life with Your Pet

1. How often do you stand still for a few moments?

2. What are the outcomes of your stumbling around in the darkness?

3. Recall an experience in which you stopped your stumbling efforts and then found something positive.

You Can Win a Copy of this Book!

Share Your Favorite Pet Pictures

Your dog in the dishwasher, licking plates.
Your cat hanging upside down on a tree limb near the bird feeder.
Your horse scratching her backside on a pole and smiling.

What's your favorite picture of your pet?

You've seen three of my favorite pictures. I want to see yours.

Share your favorite pet picture. Here's how:

✓ Go to www.ListentoLife.org/pets and upload your favorite pet picture.

✓ Identify or tag the photo and include your email address.

✓ Your name goes in a weekly drawing to win a **FREE** copy of this book!

Share Your Favorite Pet Stories

You've read my favorite pet stories. I want to read yours.

Share your favorite pet story. All you need to do is:

➢ Go to www.ListentoLife.org/pets and write your favorite pet story.

➢ Give us your email address.

➢ Your name goes in a weekly drawing to win a **FREE** copy of this book!

Listen to Life with Your Pet Greeting Cards

Now you can send your fellow pet lovers *Listen to Life with Your Pet* greeting cards. This exclusive line of cards features this book's great stories so you can share them with your friends and family, coworkers and neighbors on their special days.

And it's so EASY.

Order online at www.ListentoLife.org/cards.

There's no need to:

- Waste gas, going to the store and stand for hours picking out a generic card.
- Get in line to buy a stamp at the post office.
- Hope someone else didn't send the same card.

Here's how easy it is:

➢ Order online, customizing your card with your special thoughts and feelings, or you can use our greetings.

➢ We mail it for you!

➢ All for the cost of a store-bought card!

The *Listen to Life with Your Pet* Greeting Cards are:

✓ Convenient for you

✓ Customized by you

✓ A cost-saving value to you

We'll even remember to send a card for you to the same person when the next year's special event rolls around!

Send Listen to Life with Your Pet Greeting Cards to wish:
Happy Birthday   Happy Anniversary   New Baby
Live Positive/Motivational   Holidays   Get Well   Sympathy
Thinking of You   Thank You   Just Because   Friendship

And ONLY from *Listen to Life*, **Pet Bereavement Cards** featuring the exclusive stories you read in this book about Dr. Joey's bereavement that promise to comfort your friends in their time of loss.

We'll even send this book as a gift for any event!

Just go to www.ListentoLife.org/cards and discover how easy and inexpensive it is to send the exclusive Listen to Life with Your Pet Greeting Cards.

(We offer special volume discounts to business professionals and executives including the pet service industry. Call 1.877.4DRJOEY or email DrJoey@ListentoLife.org for details.)

Discover the Power of Your
Positive Life with Dr. Joey

For nearly three decades, Dr. Joey has coached and spoken to individuals and organizations, helping them discover how to redefine their reality and fulfill their dreams and goals by listening to life and making a positive life, not just a living, in a negative world.

To invite Dr. Joey to speak to your corporation, association, or organization, go to www.ListentoLife.org and click on "Speaking." Watch his YouTube video speaking sample and download Dr. Joey's Speaking One-Sheet to discover testimonials and the return on investment other groups discovered. Please allow plenty of time in scheduling. Special discounts are available to non-profits, particularly pet-related groups including humane societies.

To ask Dr. Joey to coach you to Perceive, Conceive, Believe, Achieve, and Receive Your Positive Life, go to www.ListentoLife.org and click on "Coaching." Select and submit a completed Coaching Interest Form. We will call you back as soon as possible. Coaching is done by phone with an appointment. Group coaching is also available.

Quantity Purchases of *Listen to Life with Your Pet* Are Available

Dr. Joey enjoys supporting pet-related agencies that promote pet adoption and spay/neuter programs as alternatives to euthanization. To lend his support in fund-raising for such organizations, he offers deep discounts on bulk purchases of this book.

Also, he offers discounts on quantity purchases to business professionals and executives who care for their customers and clients by gifting this book.

Enjoy these special offers by emailing DrJoey@ListentoLife.org or calling 1.877.4DRJOEY.

Listen to Life Like a Child is Dr. Joey's book that coaches us to listen to life like a child and make a life, not just a living. Through everyday stories about experiences he's had with his daughters and other people with their children, this book revitalizes your spirit and connects you with the joyful Spirit of God. You listen to your life and hear God say:

- "Love You!"
- "Be Good"
- "Hold My Hand"
- "Look Both Ways"
- "Play Nice"

If you want to enjoy life like a child, this book is for you!

Listen to Life, Too: The Second Book is another wonderful, widely-acclaimed collection of everyday stories that you'll read over and over again. This book inspires you to make a life, not just a living and helps you focus on what's really important in life. It's just the book you want for living right now!

Listen to Life: The First Book is the widely-acclaimed first collection of everyday stories published by Dr. Joey. They also include three "Listen to Your Life" reflection questions so that you can write your own stories about connecting with God's love.

Three Easy Ways to Buy the Listen to Life Series

1.   Call 1.877.4DRJOEY and place your order with one of our friendly associates who love talking with you, our friends.

2.   Go to www.ListentoLife.org 24/7 and order through our highly-secure, easy-to-use online store. It's really that simple!

3.   Also, order from your favorite online bookstore like Amazon.com.

If you have suggestions for more books in our Listen to Life series, email us at DrJoey@ListentoLife.org. If you'd like to share your Listen to Life stories with us, we're glad to receive them and may include them in our next book! Just email your story to DrJoey@ListentoLife.org.

If for some reason, you are not satisfied with any Listen to Life product or experience, we'll give you your money back, no questions asked.